LEARN ABOUT
OCEAN ZONES

By Golriz Golkar

Published by The Child's World
1980 Lookout Drive • Mankato, MN 56003-1705
800-599-READ • www.childsworld.com

Design Elements: Shutterstock Images
Photographs ©: Irina Markova/Shutterstock Images, cover
(ocean), 1 (ocean); Shutterstock Images, cover (jar), 1 (jar),
4 (soap); iStockphoto, 4 (rubbing alcohol), 4 (dropper),
23; Red Line Editorial, 5; Rick Orndorf, 6; Andrey Kuzmin/
Shutterstock Images, 9; Sergiy Zavgorodny/Shutterstock
Images, 10; Andrey Armyagov/Shutterstock Images, 13; Dmitri
Ma/Shutterstock Images, 14; Exploring the Inner Space of
the Celebes Sea/NOAA OAR/OER/NOAA, 17; New Zealand-
American Submarine Ring of Fire 2005 Exploration/NOAA
Vents Program/NOAA, 18; NOAA Office of Ocean Exploration
and Research/2016 Deepwater Exploration of the Marianas/
NOAA, 21

ISBN 9781503832114
LCCN 2018962804

Printed in the United States of America
PA02420

About the Author

Golriz Golkar is a teacher and children's author who lives in Nice, France. She enjoys cooking, traveling, and looking for ladybugs on nature walks.

TABLE OF CONTENTS

CHAPTER 1

Let's Make the Ocean Zones!

MATERIALS

- [ ] Glass jar with lid
- [ ] Black food coloring
- [ ] ³/₄ cup corn syrup
- [ ] Funnel
- [ ] ³/₄ cup blue dish detergent
- [ ] Blue food coloring
- [ ] ³/₄ cup water
- [ ] Oil-based blue candy food coloring
- [ ] ³/₄ cup vegetable oil
- [ ] Rubbing alcohol
- [ ] Dropper
- [ ] Stickers of ocean animals (optional)

70% Isopropyl Rubbing Alcohol

FIRST AID ANTISEPTIC

Use for:
- Topical Antiseptic & Sanitizer
- Antibacterial Cleansing Agent for Minor Cuts & Abrasions
- Preparation of Skin Prior to an Injection

WARNING FLAMMABLE — Keep away from heat, spark, electrical, fire or flame

Use only in a well-ventilated area; fumes may be harmful

Caution: Do not point at self or others; Product will squirt when squeezed

32 fl oz (1 qt) 946 mL

It is a good idea to gather your materials before you begin.

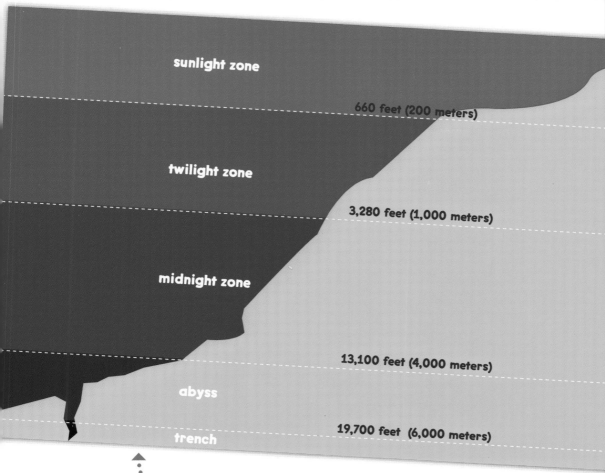

sunlight zone

660 feet (200 meters)

twilight zone

3,280 feet (1,000 meters)

midnight zone

13,100 feet (4,000 meters)

abyss

19,700 feet (6,000 meters)

trench

Ocean zones are a way of measuring depth. Each zone is very different.

STEPS

1. Put the corn syrup and black food coloring in a bowl. Mix together.

2. Pour the corn syrup into the jar. This is the trench zone of the ocean.

You will have five zones when you finish.

3. Pour the blue dish detergent over the corn syrup. Use a funnel. The layers should not mix. This is the abyss zone.

4. Add blue food coloring to the water. Tilt the jar carefully. Pour the water slowly.

Make the water run down the inside wall of the jar. This is the midnight zone.

5. Add the vegetable oil and blue candy coloring to the mixing bowl. Mix well. Slowly pour it on the inside wall of the jar again. This is the twilight zone.

6. Use a dropper to add a layer of rubbing alcohol. Ask an adult if you need help. Drip it slowly on the inside wall of the jar. The alcohol must not mix with the oil. This is the sunlight zone.

7. You can label each ocean zone on the outside of the jar. You can add stickers of the animals of each zone.

CHAPTER 2

What Is an Ocean Zone?

Each ocean zone is a unique underwater **ecosystem**. Animals and plants change to fit their zone. There is less light in deeper zones. Some zones have no light at all. The shades of blue in the project showed the amount of light per zone. The lowest zones have no light.

Light can only travel through the first two ocean zones. The bottom zones only have darkness.

Most divers can't go below 130 feet
(40 m) due to strong water pressure.

The water from the upper zones pushes down on the lower zones. This is called water pressure. The deepest zones have the most pressure. The pressure is strong enough to crush metal. Scientists build special machines to explore safely. Animals living there don't need protection.

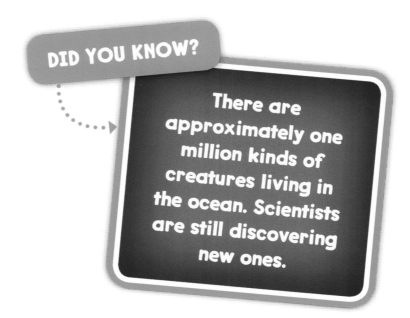

DID YOU KNOW?

There are approximately one million kinds of creatures living in the ocean. Scientists are still discovering new ones.

CHAPTER 3

What Is It Like in the Upper Zones?

The upper layer of the ocean is the sunlight zone. It reaches from the surface to 660 feet (200 m) deep. **Photosynthesis** happens here. Plants and algae absorb sunlight. They use sunlight and gas in the air to create food. Then **oxygen** is released into the air. Animals and humans need to breathe oxygen to live. Fish breathe oxygen in the water.

Many of the most recognizable ocean animals call the upper zones home.

The sunlight zone is full of life-forms called **phytoplankton**. These tiny creatures are the basis of the ocean **food web**. Some types of fish feed on the phytoplankton. Those fish are then eaten by bigger fish.

Phytoplankton are food for many ocean creatures, including whales, jellyfish, and shrimp.

Ocean birds and humans eat the big fish. Many other animals live in the sunlight zone. They include sharks, jellyfish, seals, and sea turtles.

Below is the twilight zone. It reaches approximately 3,280 feet (1,000 m) deep. The light is dim. Plants cannot survive here. Animals must handle cold temperatures. They include octopuses, squid, and hatchet fish. These animals have narrow or dark bodies. They hide easily from predators.

DID YOU KNOW?

Some animals in the sunlight zone are dark on the top and light on their undersides. They blend in if a predator tries to hunt them from below.

CHAPTER 4

What Is It Like in the Lower Zones?

The midnight zone reaches approximately 13,100 feet (4,000 m) deep. No light enters this zone. The water is very cold. Only small fish such as viperfish and frill sharks live here. These animals have big mouths and sharp teeth. They also have stretchy stomachs. This allows them to hold lots of food.

The creatures that live in the lower zones often look strange due to their harsh environment.

The growth on top of an angler fish's head glows
to attract prey in the darkness of the abyss.

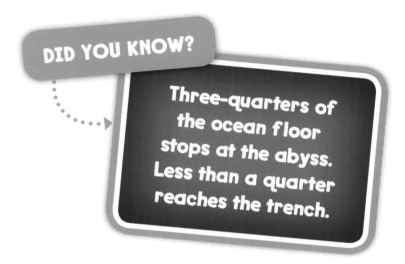

DID YOU KNOW?

Three-quarters of the ocean floor stops at the abyss. Less than a quarter reaches the trench.

The abyss zone dips to 19,700 feet (6,000 m). The water pressure is strong. Animals here are unlike any others on Earth. Many have unhinged jaws. This helps them sweep up food like a vacuum. The angler fish has a glowing body part. It attracts **prey**. Starfish and squid also live in this zone.

The deepest zone is the trench. It gets as deep as 36,000 feet (11,000 m). The water in this zone is nearly freezing. Few creatures live here. Tiny **crustaceans**, sponges, and sea cucumbers make their home here. They eat parts of dead animals and plants that sink from higher zones.

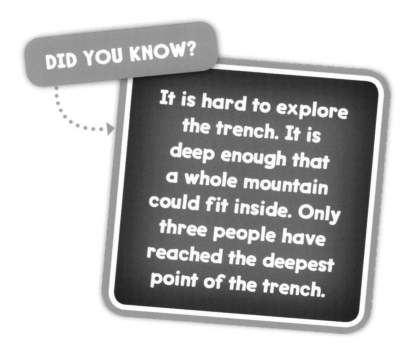

DID YOU KNOW?

It is hard to explore the trench. It is deep enough that a whole mountain could fit inside. Only three people have reached the deepest point of the trench.

Little is known about the creatures that call the trench home. Scientists often find new animals, such as this sea snail, which was first discovered in 2016.

Glossary

crustaceans (kruh-STAY-shuns) Crustaceans are animals with hard, jointed shells that live in water. Crabs, lobsters, and shrimp are examples of crustaceans.

ecosystem (EE-koh-sis-tum) An ecosystem is a community of living things interacting with their environment. The sunlight zone is the ocean ecosystem where photosynthesis takes place.

food web (FOOD WEB) The food web is interlocking food chains within an environment. Phytoplankton are the basis of the ocean food web.

oxygen (OX-i-gen) Oxygen is created by plants during photosynthesis. Humans and animals need oxygen to breathe.

photosynthesis (foh-tuh-SIN-thuh-sis) Photosynthesis is the process where green plants use sunlight to convert water and carbon dioxide into food. Phytoplankton in the sunlight zone are involved in photosynthesis.

phytoplankton (fy-toh-PLANK-tuhn) Phytoplankton are tiny plant or bacteria particles that float in bodies of water. Algae are a kind of phytoplankton in the ocean.

predators (PRED-uh-terz) Predators are animals that hunt other animals for food. Ocean birds are predators of fish.

prey (PRAY) Prey are animals that are hunted, caught, and eaten by another animal. Small fish are prey for sharks.

To Learn More

In the Library

Higgins, Nadia. *Oceans.* Minneapolis, MN: Bullfrog Books, 2018.

Kurtz, Kevin. *A Day in the Deep.* Mt. Pleasant, SC: Sylvan Dell Publishing, 2013.

Wilsdon, Christina. *Ultimate Oceanpedia: The Most Complete Ocean Reference Ever.* Washington, DC: National Geographic Kids, 2016.

On the Web

Visit our website for links about ocean zones: childsworld.com/links

Note to Parents, Teachers, and Librarians: We routinely verify our Web links to make sure they are safe and active sites. So encourage your readers to check them out!

Index